Published by Artistic Cultivation
A division of RYP LLC
Printed in the United States

A Convolution of
Emotions

— RYP —

Preface

This has been an interesting journey, and I've learned so much about myself in others. Through heartbreaks, traumatic experiences and the subsequent recovery phase, I learned how to be independent. The ironic part is that, after those painful experiences, I wanted to cling on to people.

I thought that, while being hurt, I had the capacity to love. I was in denial. It took some time, but those were crucial lessons to learn. After being hurt and stricken to my knees, I needed to learn how to pray and how to re-love myself to the extent that I would not allow myself to get to that point again. In a couple of instances, I found myself there, so low.

The older I got, the more I learned the real definition of self-love. It is subconsciously implemented that, as a woman, I cannot be selfish. And as a Latina, I must cater and nurture others. In this process, I became distant. I learned about everything and nothing.

I took out the time to heal and focus on me. I tried rewiring structures and habits that were instilled in me. I took back everything and started to feel entitled to my own life, not allowing myself to owe anything to anyone and not allowing anyone to owe anything to me. Isolation versus solitude was an ongoing battle that was happening in my head. Was I being alone by choice or was I isolating myself in fear of the world? Fear of judgment, fear of the truth. Fearing that my path wasn't as perfect as I planned it to be. Fearing that the rocks that I'd tripped over would recur in a different storyline with different people. Little did I realized that the more I feared it, the more I was manifesting it.

People began sharing their stories with me, and that's where some of these poems came about. The more I listened to people's stories, the more I was able to relate to my own poetry.

I wrote these poems in hopes of capturing everyone's attention. I'm pretty sure that we all have painful memories locked away somewhere. For those who overcame those experiences, this is simply a reminder to always remain humble and always be kind. This is not to have anyone relive their past. This is simply an encouragement to those who are undergoing painful moments in their lives, to seek help. You are never alone in your struggles. Someone out there may share a similar experience.

I had both healthy and unhealthy habits to cope with those demons. We tend to turn to substance abuse, social media, and become the toxic person we've been running away from. I set goals for myself because if I can overcome my goals while struggling, at least I won't feel like I was being held back. Sometimes we must slow down.

Seeking therapy is a great solution. I have a really hard time expressing my problems to people. I avoided therapy; I avoided speaking to my friends and family about my problems because, no matter how close you are to them, people tend to judge and give suggestions like *"you should've done this"* or *"you should've done that."* When people come to you with their problems, just listen.

Therapy works for many people, but what worked for me was exploring my spirituality and building a connection with my higher-self and God. I meditate often. At the beginning, I wasn't getting the results I was searching for. Eventually, I faked it till I made it. I found peace and ease. I learned about different religions and cultures to seek natural remedies to attract health, wealth and abundance. Gratitude taught me to be thankful for the moments I've regretted and moments

I have been praying for. Every morning I wake up saying *thank you*.

The hardest part was forgiveness. Throughout this process, I learned that forgiveness is key. It was time to forgive others, and it was time to forgive myself. To forgive how naive I was. I trusted others more than I trusted myself, placing me in danger. One of the main rules in chess, never put yourself in a predicament that'll position your king in checkmate.

There were moments when I truly thought I forgave myself but I realized I remained with the old habits of sabotaging myself. I was a great motivator and convinced people to go after their dreams even though I couldn't even motivate myself. What motivated me were my failures and how left out I felt because of my unrealistic expectations for myself. When I reached a certain level of exhaustion, I realized I had not forgiven myself, nor those who had hurt me. I started placing the blame on people who had harmed me years ago and had nothing to do with my present or future.

Poetry became my remedy. These poems were mainly written between the ages of 15 years through 23 years old. Something I do regret doing is not writing enough happier poems throughout the process. The upcoming books will hopefully be lighter and less dark poetry. But who knows? Let's see what the future has in store for me.

Contents

Sometimes pain does this to you; it makes you stronger and more beautiful than you have ever been before. It's inevitable that doubt and pain still travel through my nervous system, but I've mastered the concept of facing my fears. Vulnerable when consumed by fear, stronger while facing them.

The Right of a Woman

I have been oppressed for hundreds of years.
I have held in my emotions and tears.
I am an emotional beautiful creature.
Look at my curves and my outstanding features.
I have a womb that procreates yet I have
a portal to a man's satisfaction.
I have gentle hands and a body that will
make you tempt an action.
But that does not give you a reason to take advantage
Or to lock me down and keep me hostage.
For I have been rapped and tamed for hundreds of years.
But I stand up to you for others like me because I am fierce.
Do not take away my rights because I'm different.
Do not think that I lack experience because I look innocent.
Do not make me nurture you as if I were your mother.
Let's not clash like lightning and thunder.
I do not exceed to be more powerful than you.
I only demand freedom and equality too.
That is my right.

Requests from My Curls

You may rest your hands on my curls,
but please do not tangle them.
In every knot, a history of pain and
pleasure travels from its stem.
From its roots, you will feel its soft undefined curls
That swirl
From a tender-headed girl
That has struggled to comb her hair gently.
Using brushes so rough, looking for
curls, you can no longer see any.
The only heat allowed to be applied on
my hair is the heat of your hand.
But please be gentle.
Although it is all mental,
It has taken me years to learn I must be benign to my hair.
There may be damaged parts from what was
previous, so continue if you dare.

An Aggressive Spirit

I have an aggressive spirit,
A lineage of ancestors who were slaves and killed.
Great grandparents sacrificing themselves
for future generations.
From parents who each worked 3 jobs
at a time to maintain us.
Then you wonder why I have an aggressive spirit.
We've been silenced for so long, but I've
taken advantage of every opportunity.
I'm always working because my people
carved this pathway for me.
I'm not quiet because I speak on behalf
of those who raised me.
I demand more because that's what my people deserve.
Then you wonder why I have an aggressive spirit.
We didn't have much growing up,
But we understood the magic of making
something out of nothing.
There's magic in me, baby.
Learning to manifest every dream our souls desire.
Breaking generational curses of brainwashing
and ideologies that have oppressed us.
Embracing the drums that beat to our heartbeat, religions
that have been oppressed, the medicines that have been
rejected, the skin color that everyone looked down on.
We've lost our roots within the forest
and jungles that feed us.
Then you ask me why do I have an aggressive spirit?

I am constantly working because I have to make the
best of each moment, not for me but for the rest of us.
You may think it's a selfless thing to do, but my
people have been selfless to get me to this point.
There's love and community in places you couldn't imagine.
There are colors in the songs we chant that you can't see.
There's more than what you can imagine, but instead of
learning from our community, you choose to judge.
But then you ask me why do I have an aggressive spirit?

Subtle Fear of Losing

An urging tick,
A ticking nerve.
A touch so sick,
An ending curve
Flies away in cool cold air.
The wind blows and plays with my hair.
Lose yourself
Up two shelves.
Find a book,
Lose the nook.
Feel the touch.
Heavy much?
Heavy heart
Falls apart.
In a cold winter day,
Be prepared to stay
With me alone.
Patches are sewn
To surrender,
To the opposite gender.
Do not fear
The different sphere
But love the unknown.
Please, don't hang up the phone.

"I'm here" is all I search for in words...

Your stay.

If you present to me a sense of security, my insecurities will diminish.

If you ever see past insecurities seeping through my pores, just send a reminder:

"I'm here"

The Depth of Her Silence

She has not spoken to me;
She puts things in front of me to see.
Not one word is exchanged.
Everything becomes rearranged.
Don't know the language she speaks;
I haven't heard a sound, so I question if she even speaks.
Losing me into a track asking for what she seeks,
What if I am the one that cannot hear?
What if I am the one that cannot understand
things even if they're clear?
See, listening is a skill that not everyone has mastered.
I could barely tell if she could hear because
to my questions, she hasn't answered.
Maybe the questions I have questioned doesn't make sense,
And perhaps these questions are too intense
That give goosebumps and question your life.
These words slit my throat without a knife.
I become the silent one. These words I
hear from my mouth, silence me.
And I start to see
As if I were blind,
As if these words were too kind.
She hears more than I can, even though she's deaf.
She is more full of life, with a life full of length.
She speaks louder than I can, even though she's mute.
Because her roots burst quickly into fruits.
She doesn't wait a minute because her life is full of smiles

Whereas I complicate life and categorize
redundant things into files.
A hug is a hug in whichever language you speak.
A breath is a breath in whichever way that you breathe.
A hand is a hand wherever you place it,
And you don't have to go through life
alone, however you face it.
So I smiled back at her and hugged goodbye
Because her silence taught me the definition of being alive.

The Freedom to Dream

Dreaming
Is how we are perceiving,
And retrieving,
Reality's receiving.
See, I do not see
The fee
That you ask me to see.
Let the dreams melt
Because the reality is what I have felt
When no one knew with what I had dealt.
Dreams are our reality when planned.
Goals, a grand slam
In life's exam.
3 bases and you're home
When your brain is in the zone,
When a tone
Is no longer monotone.
Living large, outside the box
While an idea grows by kicking rocks.
Because a dream can be a daze,
A phase,
And an imaginary place,
But no need to keep it wrapped up and laced.
Go ahead and misplace
The trace,
Rewind to unwind
To then have a taste of this wine.
It is okay to draw outside the line.

I build homes in people in order to run away from my castle when it crumbles.

Dreams and Waves

So when dreams come,
Lay down next to me.
I'll be swallowed completely
By the nearby sea.
I will either be laying down,
Relaxing, floating away,
Or washed away by the waves,
Never reaching the bay.
Tonight,
I decide
To abide
To whatever life brings me,
Under a fruit tree
That will feed me
And embrace me.
My thoughts have never expanded
Out of its shell.
Lack of imagination, clicheic
Words, can you not tell?
The warmth of my love has
Overpowered
And has taught me how to be devoured.
Subliminal messages are still thrown at my face.

Running away? Am I running at my pace?
I'll keep running slower
And slower
And slower
And slower
Until I become bolder.
I smile while life humors me.
Because this calm sea
Has always and forever
Threatened me of forceful waves,
And nothing ever happens because I haven't tested the waves.

Dangerous Waves

The melody rings in my ear,
The water so rich and clear.
The ocean where the wonders linger.
The salty taste, touched with my finger.
Rises the sun and down it goes,
Decorating the beach with a natural glow.
Peaceful sight,
Wishful light.
Everyone warned me of its dangerous waves.
Countless people have turned into their slaves.
Everyone travels through its dangerous path,
But I laid on it to take a simple bath.
I ignored the world and trusted this natural beauty,
And got knocked down by one of the
deadly waves, which was its duty.
I was warned and didn't listen;
I got distracted by the way its skin glistened.
Everyone's transportation was by water.
Some souls were being slaughtered.
We opened our eyes and cried blood.
Blood mixed itself with the sand that is now mud.
I am once again free.
I'll leave you alone with your greed.

2019

Asking the person who dug you into the rabbit-hole to dig you out, it's like asking the devil to save you.

Your eyes are deceiving
And I just kept believing.

Fast but slowly the clock spins;
Time wasted and I heard violins.

2013

Out of Tune

The violin hurts me deep inside;
The strings and the bow play the tears that I've cried.
Corrupted my heart in ways I've never felt,
And somehow, slowly my body tends to melt.
When I play such a beautiful instrument,
My body automatically becomes glued to cement.
Facing an instrument that is like a living person,
Both of our conditions worsen.
The violin plays so sadly it makes everyone cry,
And slowly it kills me, and no one notices that I die.
I have to tune it every five seconds because it's cold outside,
but it's even colder where your heart resides.
My hand played the instrument with force,
But sadly, it played because my heart was led by yours.
Although its sound was amazing,
It left me as a zombie, off to dazing.

God knows that I haven't been able to forgive certain people, so He continues to put me into situations to learn how to forgive.

My best quality is being loyal;
My worst quality is expecting it in return.

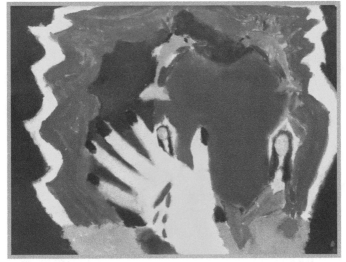

2007

Salted Wounds

Still bitter, enough to taste the salt on wounds.
Hoping that my tongue dissolves the salt
and that would shift my mood.
Bitter enough that hope slips away
quietly through my fingers.
As the last ounce of potential, hope lingers
From my fingertips without a warning sign.
Going through earthquakes and
landslides, I will still do just fine.
I pack up my bags and go before the situation worsens.
I am strong and I am me. I am my own person.

2007

The Cry of a Candle

Have you ever seen a candle cry?
Blown away by a simple sigh.
It's where the tears drip down into wax.
Where the three-branch brass accumulates wax
And is told to relax.
Depending on the occasion,
Lighting it up maybe a complication.
Have you ever seen a candle cry?
While time passes by?
When a home is a home,
The candle lights up the whole globe.
Bright
In sight,
The only light,
But at the end of the day, it still cries.
Have you seen a candle cry?

Send me flowers.

Not just any kind of flower. Potted flowers.

Send them as a reminder that we must attend to our love as long as our garden lives.

Send them on days when the desire in our hearts start to dim.

The Rising Rose of a New Era

Tonight I can hear my heart beating through my pillow,
Where the cover full of roses simply billows
Because of how much cold breeze fly into my room.
I'm just waiting for the day these roses bloom.
The poetry is dull and the painting is a mess,
But it is the heartbeat that relieves so much stress.
This breeze will kill my roses.
The love, as she composes
Dies within those weeds,
The wrong planted seeds.
She is I in third person.
Same heartbeat, but the situation worsens.
She dies and I am recreated,
And every strand, vessel, bloodstream, and cell was debated
To which stays and which goes.
These features came forth and not many rose.
You seem to ask, where is the love?
It's pushed to an edge,
As to this world, I pledge
That I am and I will give you the best of me.

Don't Judge a Storm by Its Silence; Holding It All In.

The wind that blows out of my mouth,
No one hears it.
Hurricanes come from the south,
'I ain't ignant'.
Tornado is torn apart,
Another new start
For two vicious cyclones.
A mess left alone.
It's getting to me,
These different winds blew by the sea,
By land, by me!
Lack of sleep,
Eaten away by a sheep.
Let me rephrase that, a scapegoat
That will float
On a boat
On top of the wind that slits its throat.
The cycle, we all are one.
The wind, the goat, the boat, the sun.
My words speak out until I'm done.
And it's spitting out like a waterfall in a cave.
A slave
That rides the wind of life. A rave.

Everyone's experience was different growing up. I remember being dressed in these pretty dresses. I remember having different people and different families over. I remember visiting those people as well. With each individual person, I recall developing a different bond regardless of age. For the most part, I was calm and quiet, and then I had my reckless moments. I remember that these bonds mean something. Whether they were family or not, I remember my parents referring to them as family. Everyone in our generation was referred to as cousins. So, growing up, when my teachers would ask me to create a family tree, it was all sorts of messed up. I might be too shy to approach people and pretty awkward at showing love, but I become intrigued by the slightest of things and my silence is not linked with the idea of not caring. It is actually linked with absorption. Absorbing in the moments. I miss those moments of being a child. Family and friends are family even if time and distance are in the way, even if they simply converted into memories.

The African proverb 'it takes a village to raise a child' holds high levels of significance to me. Growing up, my mother tried to keep us in a very well protected bubble. I wouldn't blame her, since the area we lived in wasn't the safest. My teachers were very motivating, which led me to stay after school. Missing a day of school felt as if the world was going to end. Even if I was sick, I'd pack up my upset stomach and marched right into class, until I was kicked out because I could be contagious. God handpicked my teachers for a reason. I always attracted the older generations in a way they would always look out for me. I had this one teacher who would always take a few students and me for lunch. She was vegetarian, and that was one of my many motivations to be vegetarian. She would take us to temples and churches to experience different religions, not to practice but to understand how everyone is different and respect everyone regardless of any background. She understood that we were low-income students, so she would buy our lunches, our prom dresses, our books, movie tickets and more as long as we earned good grades. We lost touch. There are other teachers that I can name that have left a very big impact in my heart. These older generations weren't only teachers, they were angels. I also grew up in a building where, out of kindness, I would help people up with groceries and minor chores, which had escalated into a small business. Adults would take me out to different places or even pay me. I was fortunate enough to grow up in a place where I was treated in an amazing manner. Where if I worked hard, I would gain the respect of others regardless of age. Anytime I needed something, there was always someone there to offer help. I have little angels in life that come and go. I'm extremely appreciative of everyone who has shared valuable time with me, even for a second, and I thank you. Especially those adults who have contributed in my life or still do. Even though I am a lot older, every now and then I still receive help from wiser individuals. I am still growing; I have not yet reached my full potential. I will promise to keep giving my best! I am here because I've been raised this way. I will give my kids everything they need, and if they want something, they would have to earn it someway. It is how life works; if you want something, go for it. Make sure to thank those who have given it to you!

2007

The Backbone of Backless People

I am the backbone of backless people.
I fight a thousand and one challenges as my daily sequel.
These two people are my life and run through my blood.
As these pains scar me, I soak in my tears that I flood.
Accidents that create who you are.
Accidents that rebuild you and make you go far.
Accidents that make you carry extra
weight, but make you stronger.
My swimming yards were shorter, but
this made my distance longer.

Forced things don't turn out great

My home used to be empty,
And all about it crept me.
My home was only empty because my father worked 2 jobs.
My parents worked hard so we didn't have to live like slobs.
My home was full of things for me to be entertained,
But now looking at it, I was such a fool.
My home is full,
But everything about it is dull.
My home doesn't have that home feeling anymore.
My parents are bored of sitting down; it leaves them sore.
My home is loud.
My parents argue so much, I don't think I'm proud.
My home is the silence.
It's so loud you can't hear anymore; it lost its kindness.
My home is pure,
Pure of all evil and I can't even find the cure.
See, I was so ungrateful my house flipped upside-down
And left everything with a frown.
My parents worked to give me everything, their all,
But I only wanted them, so they both faced a fall.
And now they're home and physically can't do much.
They're forced to be home, and all I wanted was their touch.
Forced things don't turn out great.
Be grateful and just wait for fate.

2006

The Guilt of a Superhero

She's alone.
Remember she's alone,
All alone!
It's like a dog without a bone,
No treats or credit has been given to her.
Her daughter is amazing, but her path is a blur.
This daughter of hers is so amazing
she's ready to save the world,
Yet we all quite know that she's just a girl.
A superhero, as a matter of fact,
With such cool speed and incredible tact.
She wants to go out and comfort everyone, and she has,
But not quite exactly you see, and time may fly fast.
She forgot her foundation;
She forgot how this was just a formation.
This was a dedication for her mother's salvation,
And she grew in frustration.
She saved the world to bring comfort for her mom,
But she forgot about her mom and slowly it became a bomb.
She wanted to show her mother the beauty, but she
was out comforting everyone other than her.
This daughter forgot about her mother.
She's alone.
Remember she's alone.
She's all alone.
She's in her room laying in her bed, her body paralyzed,
And the heart is overgrown with emotions and chastized.
Big enough to duplicate another heart.

She lays next to her husband, they will never grow apart,
But he is quite in the same condition.
Bam! She forgot about her missions.
So not only has this daughter failed
one person, but it's two now.
To show them their beauty was her vow.
Her brother at times has a brain capacity of barely one.
His actions are confusing, and he barely
knows what he has done.
He can't help himself, so now she has failed 3 people.
Now she hides alone in a sacred sanction at a steeple.
This daughter failed the three people that
inspired her to save the world,
Yet we all quite know she's just a girl.
But her mother is in her bedroom
She's alone.
Remember she's alone.
She's all alone.

Princess

In a position where it's becoming the art of letting go,
Your departure created way too many hearts to sow.
Filling in voids as if it were my masterpiece,
signing off contracts, as if this was a lease.
And your time is up. Always, your happiness
Expanded to every one of your vessels, like your uneasiness
And deadly infections that spread through
the body as you brushed off the pain,
Making sure others didn't worry as you continued to drain.
Leaving stains behind, but masking it well.
Now I'm home having to tell
Bad news to the rest of the world.
You are my Princess, my good girl.
Not having the courage to throw away your belongings,
Holding on to memories, I replay all of your recordings.
This house has never felt so empty without your howls,
And I miss your feistiness in every growl.
Your sass seeped into the hearts of others,
And thank God for allowing me to be your human mother.
I habitually call for you as I wake up. Coldest weather.
Your absence is more present than ever.
15 years I have been blessed by your existence,
Calculating my leap and this imaginary distance.
Best 15 years I could ever ask for.
Fly my princess, in Heaven, it is your time to soar.

Early 90's

My Brother's Keeper

I wish I could relate to you
The same way I used to.
Up in the clouds, away from reality,
How we ended up here baffles me.
We used to wrestle and get each other in trouble,
Always screaming "are you ready to rumble?"
I love you, please don't hate me.
Remember the days we
Had each other's back,
Did jumping jacks,
Raced each other,
And played monkey see monkey do,
because you are my brother.
My brother, my brother.
You will always be my brother
I hope this time you recover
from the wounds of life's blows,
From the reckless highs and lows,
From just the reality you are in,
From life's eternal sin.
Your reality is not mine,
And I hope you're doing fine.
I love you, please don't hate me
I will never let our differences faze me.
We did what we could,
And we did it for your good.
I love you sincerely, your youngest sister.
May the world warm you well this winter.

Sometimes It Hurts

Sometimes it hurts
To work overtime in order to break generational curses,
In order to move from social class to social class.
You were born in a time where it hurt.
From immigrant parents who didn't have
plans to have another child,
But here came you, a pre-me,
At a time where they made below minimum
wage to support a family of 5, to raise you.
Where you all resided in homes of others,
In a country where your parents and siblings weren't
accustomed to the cold. Where the cold hurt.
Spent the first coldest of winters living in basements
While experiencing asthma flares.
It hurt to breathe, but you continued to breathe
With the mind of a warrior, having nothing to faze you.
You went to school and signed yourself up for
after school programs at the age of 5,
In hopes of having peace of mind.
You went to school in hopes it would get you somewhere,
Only to find out that not many people care.
But it hurts to move from social class to social class,
To work overtime to break generational curses,
To work on your accent because, even
though you were born here,
You were taught by Spanish native speakers.

You had to work on your pronunciation because
the lower class slang embraced you.
You had to carry everyone's pain
Although you moved from social class to social class, you
still have immediate family members who live off of welfare.
Family members who depend on hard drugs.
But it hurts to move from social class to social class
Only one to graduate with a bachelor's. You were 21.
Only one to get an MPA. You were 25.
They don't compensate you what you deserve,
But you've taken it anyway.
You've asked, but they keep leaving you in the air.
You ask and pray to receive.
You're tired of overworking,
But you still are going for it, you continue
to work hard and improve your ways.
And you keep asking,
Because you have the intention of taking back what's yours!

Daily, I give thanks to my parents, even though I don't say it all the time. One day, when I have kids in the far future, I pray to God I can be at least half the parent my parents have been to me. Even to ask for such a small portion of the way they are to me, will be more than enough to raise a child. I don't just say it because they're my parents, but because of the struggles they have been through to get me where I am today. It isn't easy to raise a child, let alone three of us. I was born in a time right after they migrated from the Dominican Republic. Cohabitating in other people's homes wasn't easy. They managed to take us out of that lifestyle. Although we didn't have much money, being poor was nothing but a mentality.

I feel that any mistakes that I have done, I should quickly correct it; I just want to make them proud. Sometimes we don't make the wisest choices, but for them, I promise to be conscious of my actions, and for them, I will use the words they preach to us. I'll apply those words to life. Their prayer is to see the best for us and to see us progress. Here's to them, my most sacred blessings.

2019

I have neglected my intuition many times.
Had I done otherwise, I wouldn't have faced half the battles I've gone through.
Listen to your inner self, listen to your inner Bruja!

My Past Match with the Devil

A bitter taste found me so sweet.
Please, I beg you to get me off my feet.
It's the reason why the Devil is after me.
Chase me as fast as you can
Because it's not on God's plan
To be loved by the Devil,
I have not yet been a rebel.
Run, run, he is after you now.
He wants you to exchange your vows
With him. He wants to buy your soul.
He wants to buy you whole.
Run with me, I know the way.
He's been after me before, you shouldn't stay.
He'll belittle your thoughts;
He'll enlarge your faults
And crumble you into a childish nightmare,
Into a world that's never fair.
But who's to say this world was ever fair.
I'll stare into those eyes without emotion,
Perplexed at false devotion.
Don't fall for his lies, I yell.
He'll capture you under his spell.
Run, run, I say.
You shouldn't stay.
This sky was once blue.
The childish innocence you outgrew.
It's gray, it's gray. The clouds are gray.
Come with me, you shouldn't stay.

Testing Faith

I hold my pain in this rosary.
I hold it very close to me.
Secrets and pain I will forever take to the grave,
Praying to God to give me the strength to be brave
Enough to continue to stay afloat.
Before I sink and it slits my throat.
The ink in this pen is what he bleeds.
You can only move forth if you believe.
The pen itself can deceive,
And weak bonds can cleave.
That is only if it is not strong enough.
Keep moving forward even if it gets rough.

Suicidal Veins

My creativity has vanished.
Trembling illusions hide for it cannot be managed.
Sweat goes down through the veins my blood once traveled.
It's clear now where biology doesn't
make sense, and I am baffled.
Sweet dreams that have lied to me.
Darkened nights in which I have drowned into a deep sea
Of blood, darkened blood, and maybe I found this is where
My sweat kicked my blood out into what I now stare
And slowly drown. Drowning in what has made me,
Faced me,
Played me,
And perhaps even saved me.
Planning out the sorts of decisions to choose from,
Dipped into a level of alcohol beyond the rum.
Life surpassed fear,
And I am the driver of the wheels that I steer.

Caged: Everyone Thinks You're Okay

Turbulence that leaves you jittery,
Exposing all your true vulnerability.
Naked, impatient, and everyone is staring.
Just being in that position is daring.
Poetry cannot heal wounds, but I can pretend.
Tainted souls and broken pieces are hard to amend.
You then become the host of a freak show,
'A woman with a morphed heart' without a beau.
Morphed heart due to radiation exposure.
Caring too much, but attempting to maintain composure.
Loosening a grip on composure
exposes her freak like actions,
But no one knows full details of such transactions.
Therefore, people who analyze her think of her as a beast,
But no one knows that the deformation of her heart ceased.
No heartbeats, a steady line on an electrocardiogram.
Living without a heartbeat, failing the humane exam.
So she writes her immortal experiences,
Portraying such depth and seriousness
To blend in and avoid being observed.
Protecting her thoughts, remaining reserved.

2006

Sometimes I fear mirrors. I don't mind looking at someone or something through a mirror, but I fear looking at me. I don't like that intense look I give myself. I don't do it on purpose, and sometimes I wonder if I give that same intense look to others. It's that intense look in which I am trying to read myself. It's a strong connection between my soul and my reflection. The problem is my soul is not ready to accept that connection. It has nothing to do with my body. The mystery lies within my eyes; it lies within my soul. It's not a bad thing. I speak to life with closed eyes and life speaks to me in a soft whisper. I attempt to speak to life with open eyes and all I hear is silence. There is no need for life to speak because it is my eyes that see everything.

I fear mirrors because I judge myself ruthlessly. Have I judged you in the same manner?

Stepping Back from The Edge

I recall the precise date and time when I lost my mind.
In front of me, my present crushed
open as I watched it unwind.
I remember developing trust issues,
hate, and unbelievable pain.
This is just me going down through memory lane.
Is there a sense of regret? Yes, there is!
But as I smoke this cigar, I endure a sense of bliss.
Life is not perfect, nor will it ever be.
I lost respect for the capabilities of what
some humans can achieve.
But that should never refrain me
To create and establish foundations for me.
Never allow your circumstances to cloud your ability to see
Into the future.
Be the seamstress that amends every incision at the suture.
I've developed a stronger mentality of growth,
But as well as living life to the fullest
and as long as I do both,
no one can tell me otherwise.
I'll let you be the witness of an empire I shall legitimize.

Trust Issues

It's usual to see this kind of issues.
The type of trust issues that have been
rooted into your imagination.
Psychedelic infiltration
Of the brain, traumatizing the cells into
believing the worst of you.
So your body acts against you
at times, when memories seep through
the cracks of your brain.
You write, dance and attempt to love just to stay sane.
You feel the love coming, simultaneously
holding hands with blockage.
You push away whatever pleasures come from
growth, experiences and knowledge.
Remember it's deeply becoming a part of you alongside fear.
Whatever happened to this strong woman
capable of moving mountains as she steered
The heavy loaded trucks that passed through them?
She survived the casualties of life and
continues to find herself
On her own. The identity of oneself.
Of what makes her amazing.
The struggle she's facing
Makes her stronger.
She's nowhere near a goner.

Trust Issues, Part Two

See, I don't know what to write about.
My mind is flawed throughout.
My heart is the author, but my mind is the editor.
My pen is my friend, but the nerve is the predator.
My legs are too slow, but my words create a path,
And to buy my heart, you have to let go of that wrath.
Should I write about your love, my love or ours?
Or maybe about how the sun shines even on rain showers.
Should I write about my moms and pops?
And to know how they are, my heart stops.
Seize the moment, stop the writing, enjoy what you've got.
The Sahara Desert is freezing cold, and Alaska is raging hot.
The moon is shining brightly, and the
sun is dimming out slowly.
God became your worst enemy, and the devil became holy.
Karma is my number one bitch, so
watch it, she's out to get you.
Or me. Who knows? Just cherish the moment like I do.
Don't hurt, and if you fuck up, apologize and make up for it.
Because having Alaska hot and the
Sahara Desert frozen does not fit
In the picture with my asthma, breathe in and breathe out.
Your brain will filter your thoughts of evil and doubt,
But your conscience will remain.
Clear it up, make up for it before it stays the same.
But remember I have nothing to write about
Because my mind is flawed throughout.

2008

Battles of Judgement

Silence! Because useless words overcrowd actions.
Unstable mindset and unawareness
of your doings are fractions
That I cannot comprehend.
Actions that I cannot commend.
Yet another beautiful action overflows, but I find no balance.
It's a beauty and a curse, but I cannot endorse malice.
A dark bright sky does not exist.
Questioning actions in which I should persist.
Have I gone mad?
Promoting emotions as if it were an ad,
Suppressing negative feelings and choosing happiness.
Living life with such cold distraction by the rapidness.
For I smile to see the day of pure joy,
And I silence myself to play the role of a lady who's coy.
What does society say?
A role in words and a silenced play?
What fun is that?
I play that part with a missing hat.
A lost tool,
A silenced heart that cannot rule.
I am the queen of my throne;
It is written all over my stone.
I am no better than anyone,
But to my soul, heart, and mind, I have won.
Due to your acts of silly play,
Your words and actions have no say!

Sometimes regret lingers deep on my mind.
That's when a bitter taste on my
tongue, I happen to find.
I question how certain things happened,
And that causes me to be so damaged.

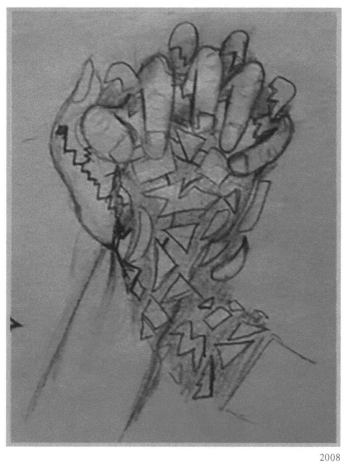

2008

Treating Negative Thoughts
Like Misbehaved Children

My frustrations
Lead to devastation.
Has your mind pondered out for some contemplation?
Spoken words while actions are lost,
Feeling the insides of your wounds and realizing that it's soft.
You are soft.
The texture of a pillow nesting a brain,
Trying to keep yourself sane
While nesting in someone else's brain.
You comfort it and listen to every word it says.
More is less
And less is more.
So it cancels out your brain
So you can only listen to its train of thought,
But remember you're soft.
Your words do not have a sense of value.
You must release yourself and become brand new.
Revaluate your thoughts become your own person.
You must stop this chain before it worsens.
Hug and love yourself like never before.

Never sell yourself and take yourself
out of display in any store.
Apologize to the wounds you gave yourself
without the intention of doing so.
Walk slow,
Repair yourself and glow.
Love, and upon arrival, you must bestow
A gift to enjoy life.

Substance Abuse

Walking in a dark room,
Avoiding my tomb.
Dancing with Johnny Walker, but seducing Jack Daniel's.
Dealing with detrimental issues, far from the granule.
She dances alone and needs the company of no one
She's not afraid to pull a trigger on a gun,
Tequila, my friend. She runs down harshly,
But she'll definitely give you a welcome at her party.
Mama Juana doesn't stand alone; she will
make you feel the presence of this earth.
She will give meaning to your birth
And why you are here to celebrate.
She will allow you to accelerate
Proceedings of any conquest or mission you have in mind.
My dearest Moët, scavenge through the
past to see what you can find.
Enhancing the urge of sending the wrong text,
And ultimately seducing the wrong person for sex.
If I ever seal my lips into a cup to whisper my secrets,
I'll have to make sure I have formed my allegiance.
Be careful when you integrate them into a gathering
Because I already hear them chattering.

Reclaiming My Strength

Before my dreams awaken every scent,
I'll pray to God and only to him I'll vent.
There are moments in circulation that must end.
Moments of regret that to my knees I bend.
Facing fears has made me stronger,
But it has made my walks difficult and longer.
I find myself in a house of worship.
I question every day, was it worth it?
To place myself in a predicament
I cannot escape. I became his equivalent
By following his lead, disguised as an angel,
Leaving my life unbalanced and unstable.
In remembrance, my legs may be trippy and wobbly,
But I have hands with a good grip and a
smart mind to think consciously.

2005

The Romance I imagined

The romance I imagined
Began lifetimes ago, but invited itself in
this lifetime at a simple glance.
The romance I imagined
Easily gave space to both of us, calm winds
passively directing us to one another.
The romance I imagined
Welcomed us into a home where memories
filled the place with love.
The romance I imagined
allowed us to find each other in different parts of the world
where the tongue wasn't ours, but we understood each other.
The romance I imagined
Appreciated our flaws, embraced them
and helped us improve them.
The romance I imagined
Gave us space to walk away after each argument
and choose each other at the end of the day.
The romance I imagined
Curled itself up into each other's chest as a
reminder that our heartbeat is one.
The romance I imagined
Was a simple emotion of happiness.

The romance I imagined
Came in the form of a flower as an invitation to your heart.
The romance I imagined
Was simple.
The romance I imagined
Didn't require maintenance.
The romance I imagined
Was understanding.
The romance I imagined
Was filled with beautiful emotions that learned to love
the broken areas of your heart that hadn't been mended.
The romance I imagined
Changed my perspectives of love.
The romance I imagined
showed past the superficial phase in which many have failed.
The romance I imagined
Turned out to be a simple imagination

Lack of Transparency

Oh, how much do you wish we were all transparent?
Where intentions blossom and are apparent
To the naked eye.
On this bed, she lies.
I mean, you lie
Too.
But she's not afraid to lie with a liar
In a bed that you acquired
At a cheap discount store.
The audacity to call her a whore
Because she is a woman who loves herself dearly.
And her faith is powerful, always doing things sincerely.
A believer, such a believer she trusts a fabricator of lies.
But she waits till God gives her a sign to cut all ties
With the man who calls her a whore.
But aren't you the whore, for
Associating yourself with other women in other beds?
And with that being said,
Why is she a whore in the first place?
Is it because your subconscious leaves you a bad taste,
When you lay down with her after being with others?
And she believed you every time you
lied while being with lovers.

Why do you change her ways,
Battle scars and wounds she will face?
No appetite, no sleep or too much sleep,
A wound that cuts so deep.
She isn't hurt by the small man that you are.
She definitely doesn't hurt because she swung you far.
She hurts because she was gullible and let her guards down.
All she wanted was love, so she let
you step on her, and a frown
Came about after realizing the world isn't transparent.

The Gullible Mind of a Rebound

Let me walk with you through the rain,
Mixed emotion through the pain.
Dark cloudy night,
The coldness with the fright.
You're not alone, you're with someone that's not me.
But let me walk you through the rain
and show you what I see.
Struggling with endless hope,
Pulled away by her rope.
But I'm here for you and it's terrifying.
I don't know whose heart will end up dying,
So let me help you uphold my hand
Because our love is what our hearts demand.
Show me the unknown and be there for me when it rains.
Hold my hand, remember me and
eliminate her from your brain.
Touch my heart in ways you already have and haven't.
Let's scream our names in the rain and make it a habit.

Effort

I want effort,
The type of effort that I would never have to ask for.
The type of love that flows fluidly.
But all you seem to know is how to act cluelessly.
I want the type of love that I've been missing all of my life.
Because you seem to love a pretty face, but don't
know how to dig deeper into the soul.
To devour me whole,
Mainly mentally,
And experience all that happiness, chemically.
To take out the time to learn me,
To observe me,
And embrace my flaws.
And when issues arise, I'll know who to call.
For comfort, for ease.
The love that gets you weak in the knees.
But you just don't love anymore,
And at this point, there's a lot to restore.
Luckily, there's a line of men and women
out there waiting for me.
We can never seem to find a middle point and never agree.
I hate to say things in that manner,
But I'm lowering my standards
By just sticking around in hopes
That you fall in love with me again.
You're dragging me down, and I need to ascend.
Messaging your exes got me all types of messed up,
And solely your presence is definitely not enough.

They tell me to let go of my fears, but my fears continuously lead me back to you.

Just note that the insecurities that flow within me aren't mine; they were instilled unto me by a *pendejo*, but I have to own up to it because I allowed it.

The Mind Will Play Tricks on You

How deep lies the magic of your wounds?
Scabs are the burial of the past, and above there is a tomb
Of all broken promises that nurtured pain.
Illusions became reality, and reality kept me sane.
Above it all, I rise to the scent of fresh hope.
I wash my fears with blessed lukewarm water and soap.
The driven mentality of moving forward surprises
The persistent demons that fantasizes
With oppressing me,
And the darkness surrounding me.
I smile because, even though they are after me,
My faith is powerful beyond measures.
See, I count my treasures,
And it surpasses any negativity that hell has placed
On my soul.
Let it rock and roll.
Let it celebrate.
Because I'll reinstate
My affirmation to its end.

When You Notice, It's Time to be Alone

Cinnamon swirls of misery.
Moments left an after taste that's bitterly
Sweet. But the cycle is vicious,
Momentarily delicious.
Once you realize it's a game,
Continue to make the same
mistakes, over and over.
Noticing these patterns when sober,
But you're drunk all the time.
Saying words like 'but I know he's mine'
When clearly he's not
And you never were his. He meant a lot
To you, but he didn't seem to reciprocate
These feelings. To demonstrate
Any kind of loving emotions he failed to do.
Technically, he never failed to show you
Because those were far from his intentions.
The on and off cycle attracted the same men.
Inconsistent invites, time and again.
These attractions are manifested from your frequency.
You start to wonder if men happen to have any decency?
You need a break from anyone entering your aura,
Especially the amount of fuck boys that enter in plethora.
Each time, one leaves a scent behind
To attract the next one in line.

When people bring more negative things in your life than positive, more cons than pros, if they break you apart each time, **let them go.**

Not for anyone else but for you. I think that's the type of spring cleaning I've had this year. We all need people, but the pain is what I'm learning to let go of. It's probably one of the hardest things, especially when the pain has kept me company for the past couple of years.

2009

*P*oetry that exasperates emotions.
I reread them softly into the present,
Hoping it vanishes as it attempts to
Walk into the future.

Going in With a New Perspective

It grew like a tree
Requiring a fee.
A seed to my chest,
And it grew to the best.
A full-blown heart it became,
And my body never stayed the same.
You were in me, and you were my heart.
In my chest, guaranteed to never grow apart.
But this guarantee lied to my chest,
So I guess to my body it was a test.
This new heart grew in me, and my body rejected it
My body enjoyed the heart till the heart attacked it.
So my body died,
But the soul and the mind stayed alive.
My body died from a hole in my heart,
But revived because the hole wasn't as
abnormal as I thought from the start.
See, we think we died, but it's only the beginning.
These moments will create new hearts and
different moments to relive in.
The mind will never give up nor the heart.
It'll appear that way to find its weak
spot, and from there it starts.
To grow and strengthen that spot,
The heart becomes independent and
fights what the mind cannot.

2009

*W*hat is it that awakes the vulnerable item beyond your breast? Why do you have a cage that surrounds it made out of ribs? What's in there that makes you grow with every subtle smile that makes you want more? It's the heart that's so fragile and arouses the bloodstream with every pump. A smile makes a huge difference; it makes all simple things extravagant. So, smile!

The Purpose of a Rib Cage

My rib is supposed to protect my heart from any harm,
So why does a protected heart keep on breaking?
You're a magnet, attracting my heart with your charm.
Why does our relationship keep on shaking?
My breasts are too small to protect such big heart,
And it has gotten to a point where
my heart is all open to you.
It's a confusing situation where it's an abstract art,
And looking at different directions is the best thing to do.
Save my heart before you end up breaking it into pieces.
Save my mind from only thinking of you
when I'm supposed to save the world.
The line in my heart rate monitor keeps decreasing,
and a soothing whisper comes close to my ear,
"don't think too much and rest, young girl"

A Craftsperson

I am a painter, so I ask for you to take
away my brush and canvas.
I also am a poet, so please take away my pen and paper.
I am an explorer, so please take away my atlas.
My fashions are taken away too, so I'm
naked for you to feel my vapor.
Stay close, don't go far.
All my organs and body parts are protected except my heart.
It pumps faster than a speeding car,
Yet my body will never move, so my heart
is unprotected to even start.
My heart has been shattered a thousand and one times,
And in all the possible hard ways, I still don't learn.
But I feel that changing because of a
man is one of the worst crimes,
So the other can get what he earns.
It's not fair to treat him differently right
away because of a past mistake.
He should get a fair trial, and as innocent as
my heart is, it knows how to repair itself.
It has learned how to sense when the
shatter comes before it breaks,
So then it can start weeping before time, and right
after, like a wound, it'll start to relieve itself.

Love will not hurt me, so I'll patiently
wait for true love to find its way.
Hopefully, love is you.
My heart is naked, no ribs to protect it, so don't
descend it because for my heart I'll pray.
Be careful with the decisions you do.
So, world and your mystical forces, just give me the cue.
My heart isn't fragile, it just needs protection from you.

Diving Into Words

Showers are great, but baths are to explore me.
I will give the best of the best that is, if you don't ignore me.
I will dedicate poems to you while blushing,
I will create something.
Rose petals, something simple.
Against the water, they smoothly ripple.
Amaze me with a story, so I will not need to get a book.
Never judge a book by its cover, so I'll
read your lips without a look.
Unbiased statements to your history I'll follow,
Embracing every drop of water, even though it's shallow.
Wait until we own a lake.
Until then, I will dive into every word without a break,
Waiting for your love, to see what we can make

Assuming Your Wounds

It took me so long to love my body, and I did.
I met you and I forgot every single life
lesson I'd learned about self-value.
I have devalued myself within your presence.
I learned to hate myself, every part of it, not because of
the things you said but what you instilled in me: lies. Lies
that can never compensate the truth I was searching for.
Although at this point it is all mental, the scars
you left in me cannot seem to find love.
I've learned to love myself again.
I've learned to love parts of me I hated, but I can
never seem to find love in others due to fear.
That's the type of fear you left behind.
The type of fear and baggage I can't seem to let go of.
The type of fear a five-year-old has while shivering
under the blankets because she knows the monster
underneath her bed is out to get her.
Paranoia and fear of judgment.
Always fearing that the rest of the
world will never accept me.
I know you'd fought your own battles.
I know the battles you fought were not easy.
Slowly your battles became mine.
I trusted you with my life.
I guess it was my fault for trusting.
I won't ever again make myself the victim,
and I will keep my head up.

Poetry Misses you

The poems miss when you were in love
Constant poetry.
Your poems were always up on the latest tea
Because you were so open to write
So creative.
So invested.
So committed.
Now you work so hard?
All for what?
But when you were in love,
You couldn't wait to get home
And fall deep into meaningful conversations.
Poetry misses you, you know?
Do you remember when you painted, habitually?
You bump into your books of poems all the time;
It's a sign.
Poetry misses you.
Do you remember when was the last
time your bed was sacred?
It got to the point where you barely lay on it
Because sleep misses you too.
Do you remember the last time
You honestly felt love radiating immensely?

Such a strong feeling that you were able
to solely focus on the now.
Do you remember the time when it was so easy to write,
As if it were your calling?
Please tell me you remember.
Before the heartbreaks.
Do you remember then,
When you were
So deeply entangled
And madly in love with yourself?

2009

Ownership

Ironically, the only person I seem to confide in is you,
and for that reason, I've cut those wires of dependency.
It may seem as if you're a monster; however, I like to
believe that you were placed in a predicament of life
Where you are stuck in between rocks and ruthless waves.
I've forgiven you a long time ago,
If that is what worries you.
I wish you could make things better.
I know that statement is a complete lie, since
there is nothing you can do to reverse things.
I appreciate myself so much that, no
matter how far down I've fallen,
I never managed to let go of my goals.

The soles of my shoes do not trace the places I've traveled; I change those constantly. The bottom of my feet can tell you stories that my shoes cannot. It can tell you the moments I've stepped on shit, walked on mud, landed on hard concrete after a high jump, stomped with anger, tiptoed, danced, twirled around and fell. I fell deep into love, and my hand then wrote endless stories.

To Revive

I had not kissed someone in such a long time,
But you kissed me. The taste of tequila and lime
Lingered from your lips to mine.
I guess you got too close to unwind
the stress of life. I should not have given it, but I did for a bit.
A kiss that may lead to the need of a first aid kit.
Scratching a scab off an unhealed wound,
It's not your fault that previous predators
have left me marooned.
Although you're not seeking something serious,
Let's keep it real and let's avoid being oblivious.
I cannot allow myself to lose myself in you.
I cannot allow losing you in me.
It is a bit complicated, you see.
I must heal before I play these games.
I am not really into games, but there
are things I cannot tame.
Loving myself is more than enough, so how can
I take away from my love to give to you?
I'm definitely not ready to lay here next to you.
I have secrets and pain that I will take to the grave.
Another genuine kiss I cannot accept, but whatever
I took from that one, I will forever save.

*I*f your heart is cold, I'll dress accordingly.

The night-time reversed the thoughts of you so clearly that anything that clouded my mind spoke louder than a thunder to clarify the rays of uncertainty.

Hydrate

You have awakened a dead soul
With no intentions and no goal.
I need no one, and my happiness solely
relies on me and my attitude.
But you have awakened my soul, and
for that, I show you gratitude.
You have made love to my soul with your kind words;
It's like a homemade remedy, medicinal plants, and herbs.
I've tried to write poems before, but it wasn't the same.
Certain circumstances were unbearable and to blame
Before I could write endless poems of
everything and all kinds of deep shit.
And then dehydrated I was, and not even a verse could I spit.
Therefore, It's a celebration, let's get lit.
You moved me to a point where wounds
and scars never existed.
Positive vibes with great minds never
would like to dismiss this.

Traveling Feet

Love speaks of me and articulates every
heartbeat he skips within a sentence.
To love me, he screams these words
loudly without any repentance.
He listens closely to what my love may
have to offer and what it may not.
He has traveled the world with heartbreaks, but now
he sees a woman, someone he has always sought.
A strong woman who is comfortable
enough to feel vulnerable
Right next to him. She notices her heart is just as recoverable
As his. They've traveled the world in search of each other,
And both hearts have been accustomed to usher
Each other to the right path.
There are hard moments, but they
understand each other's wrath.
Compassion and strong feelings erode past regrets.
Taking moments to rewind and fast forward like cassettes.

In case I've ever forgotten, I'm a badass. I'm made out of flesh and bones; I'm human, and I have the same needs everyone in this world has. I'm capable of great things. Although everything has been a challenge lately, I know I got this. I know I can do this. This is for all of you guys who need a little motivation: you are also a badass, and your current circumstance does not define who you are!

Exhaustion: the only torture you succumb to in exchange for the betterment of yourself!

Hustle but Align

You want to go back to a time when simplicity
roared in excitement to want more.
Now you are on the road to extravagances, but all you
can do is scream for little things like your warm bed.
An ambitious mindset will pay off.
Sometimes all you need is balance,
But being impatient makes it even harder.

As I sat here, generating a random thought of Adam and Eve, I questioned it completely. God's intentions for both Adam and Eve was for them to eventually become mortals. You are not going to tell me that two people, who are immortal, roaming around in Paradise and prohibited to go near the forbidden tree, are not going to be curious one day to learn more about it. God wanted to test humans to see how long it would take for Adam and Eve to eat the forbidden fruit. Because had I been in that situation, already being told I would never die, eventually I would want to go to the tree and learn more about its existence.

Cradled Emotions

I want my emotions to be cradled,
Yet every inch of me is abled
To love and caress all parts of me.
But please love me weak until I drop to my knees.
My emotions will be looking up at you,
Thanking every part of you as if love was overdue.
Happiness presented itself in the form
of your body, mind and soul
Because you are the only one who has
been able to love me whole.
My emotions scream to be cradled and
welcomed into your heart
Because my inner demons were silenced and fell apart
At a glance into your eyes.
How did this happen? Please advise.
They say time is an illusion, so if that's
the case, I must be mental
Because the distance and time are
treating me far from gentle.
Please cradle my emotions
Through aligned motions.
Your kisses are potions.
Got me believing life is a dream within
a dream, an inception.
Lips that are like magic, transforming perceptions
To the point where the happiness you gifted me, radiates
through my skin and brings about happiness onto everyone.

Got me thinking wild thoughts,
praying about our future son.
A family, a house, a home
Because you treat me like a queen in her throne.
No need for sage or crystals, our love is enough.
I'm craving for you to come home and cradle
my emotions because life is too tough.
I had a rough day, and although I made
it seem as if you live miles away
By begging you to cradle my emotions and stay,
The last time I saw you was just yesterday
And honestly, that's how it feels not to
have you for a couple of hours.
Without you, my time is sour.
Please cradle my emotions because
your touch has been missed.
I'm waiting for you to get back so I can
experience again that kiss.

In The Middle of a Masterpiece

Focusing on each part to sketch,
Noticing the rough parts on each edge.
Analyzing the overall, I could tell life wasn't easy
Based on the crevices of your scars;
they've been parted so deeply.
What a gaze! It's there where secrets are hidden;
It hides every word you try to say that your mouth didn't.
As I try to add color, I see uneven tones.
Burnt marks from the sun in different zones.
I let the pencil take the lead on this one.
A wide nose that curves and attracts all the sun.
A full beard that takes time to grow and causes wit.
I wonder how many pensive thoughts have caressed it.
Lips, you could tell these lips don't say much.
I wonder when was the last time that
with lipstick they were smudged,
By other lips that aren't mine.
Perhaps it's not my time.
Moving down to his neck, shoulders, arms, and hands.
Palms so coarse and large they seem to expand.
My heart fits perfectly there.
I let you stand there as you stare
Directly into my direction,
And I let out all of my confessions.

"You look more beautiful when you smile."
"You should pour out your heart and not wait a while."
"Those eyes have secrets that I'm interested in discovering"
"Your chest is heavy, and I know you're still recovering."
"My scars are just deep as yours because
the sun has loved me the same way,
Burning me and leaving behind a beautiful
complexion that's here to stay."
"Please stay the night.
Allow me to invite
You to see, what I see in you."
These expressions of emotions are long overdue.

Batman

I'll provoke the Gotham police to
activate the Bat searchlight.
For on this dark night I want to cause a fight.
I'll race you in my cat-illac into a dark alley.
I'll show you my true self, I'll make you call me Halle.
For my fighting techniques are very aggressive yet sensual,
Bruce, daddy, I hope you know my credential.
I'll let you touch my whip if I can touch yours.
You decide I can make love or cause wars.
I know I've been naughty, but if you help me, I'll be good.
We can fight some crime together as it should.
Convince me that I'm not evil, and I'll
unbuckle your utility belt.
If you refuse to succumb, I'll duct tape you unto
the wall and bring the heat till you melt.
I'll find a way to your Bat-cave,
And I'll promise to behave.
But if you don't want me to, I can also disobey.

Sex

I'm not here to talk about religion, money or politics.
I won't talk about controversy or anything that's a quick fix.
I want to talk about lovemaking at its most passionate level,
And just because it's lovemaking does
not mean it has to be gentle.
You may see it as rough sex,
But I prefer to see it as an aggressive
man breaking every part of me
While exploring my soul and simultaneously
Surpassing my internal organs.
As he leaves, he'll pick up the pieces that he has broken,
And perhaps he'll also pick up the
pieces other men have broken.
He'll mend them together, tugging my hair
to bring me closer to his breadth
And embracing my slight laughter and my complex depth.
He understands that there's more to me than just sex.
And as we come
To the conclusion,
We'll embrace each other's presence,
Appreciating every word and every sentence
That comes out of our mouths,
And the moans or any other sounds
That our body has created.
This is a moment we both have awaited.

The Beginning Thought
of a Situationship

I want to tell you a secret,
But the challenge is, can you actually keep it?
You give me tingles in places I can't ignore,
Leaving me wanting a whole lot more.
But if you read this poem, it wouldn't make a difference.
You'll enjoy my touch, but that's just an inference.
I'm a little playful, but you like to have fun.
I tend to be serious, and I carry a heavy
heart that weighs a ton.
See, I'd like to touch you because our
hearts were left to wrestle;
I thought so much about it that I swear I popped a vessel.
The look in the eyes and the biting of the lips,
It feels like if this is The Twilight Saga: Eclipse.
But if I told you all of this, could you act as if unsaid?
Will you think of me while lying lonely in bed?
Think of the goosebumps and the shivers,
Which leave me all excited like rapid clashing rivers.
See, the feelings I have inside me are pure confusion,
But maybe they are all illusions.
You just want to play,
But all I have to say
Is that I've had a good time too.
Just remember I'm thinking of you.

Listen to Silence

Silence speaks louder than words.
If you listen intently, it will tell you
everything you need to know.
Sit still and it'll tell from its future, present to past.
A lot about someone's past.
The present is composed of past events forming that silence.
Silence doesn't mention the future if
it's future is stuck in the past.
The past always seeps through the crevices of
silence, and silence can become hard rock cold.
See, my anxiety refuses to listen to silence.
Too many voids have been explored there,
where anxiety has originated.
Not the first, and maybe not the last, but it seems as if
everyone's silence builds up forming into a black hole.
A galaxy of disappointment.
Silence creeps up to me worse than any horror story I know.
It's as if this void was composed of other's
pain and I had to deal with it.
Words are comforting, but it means nothing without action.
So it seems as if people have nothing to offer anymore,
Realizing that the more they speak, the
less they can live up to their words.
They comfort themselves in silence.
Not out of anger, not out of hate, simply
because genuinely their mind is elsewhere.
Somewhere in the past.

I mean, I hate to break it to me, but it's the truth. It's a
continual pattern of people wanting to be in the past.
Maybe my experiences weren't so sweet to ever
want to linger there, so I can't seem to relate.
I'm stuck in a generation of the past, and
I only want to move forward.
This void retains silence; the type of
silence I can see from a mile away.
The type of silence that, although I am
hopeful, it never seems to dismiss itself.
Ingesting silence as a form of a sign.

Finding A Home in a Foreign Land

Sweet phrases like *'mi amor'* or *'cariño'* awaken
Your soul and slowly start filling parts
in your heart that are vacant.
She says these phrases out of custom and affection.
Through these subtle sweet words, you find a connection.
It reminds you of your childhood, how
mamá would soothe you to sleep.
It reminds you of times when your mother
would soothe wounds that were too deep.
She calls you *'malcriado'* o *'pendejo'* because
you choose not to listen in the first place.
But she chooses these words because the deep
wounds is the punishment you'd have to face.
These terms remind you of home,
She reminds you of home.
She allows you to time travel to blissful moments.
The sound of her voice mixing with these words,
disassemble you and divide you into components,
Allowing you to feel like new all over again.
Her voice changes your soul, and she becomes the Zen
of your intuition, straining away all the
damage you have ever felt,
Pushing away any pain this world has weighed on you.
You feel like you were never a part of a diaspora
because her tongue makes you feel like home.

*H*er accent resonates in you, finally feeling at home in a
land that is foreign in which you roam.
You are no longer a foreigner because she sings the song,
And as long as you are with her, you will always belong.

Slowly Releasing Fear

So soft like a pillow and a marshmallow
Is the sensation I feel when I kiss this young fellow.
Such intense kisses that I don't seem
to find a grip to this handle.
Fear whispers so soft, like his lips. My
angels may need to light up a candle.
I feel the passion, but I'm blocked up by fear.
It's like I'm going in the right direction,
but I lose control as I steer.
Why did I endure the pain that whipped me till this day?
I hope my insecurities doesn't push him away.
I'm not ready for a lot of things, but I'm willing to try,
Slowly walking on my scale that measures distance.
Resistance has laid down next to me, but
it's frightened by my persistence.
A kiss that soothed all the pain but made me vulnerable.
Insecurities that seeps through my
pores, but I am recoverable.
I have feared life for a bit too long now,
but I am ready for change.
And to the devil, I want my soul back.
Rearrange the exchange.

So I realized that I've subconsciously sold myself short, which has lead people to act according to my subconscious views. Not anymore, hun. #Islay

Finally Understanding

In and out, I'm beautiful. I don't need you,
But I want you,
And in order to live, I don't need to want you.
The sky will be blue or grey with or without you.
My emotions were beyond my control,
And front row seating to your feelings I enrolled.
But I realized I have a brain to control my feelings.
I didn't use it; I forgot how to construct
things, and down fell my ceiling.
Above the clouds past the winds near the gates,
I still believed in Cupid, and after all,
we kept on with massive debates
On how my ceiling
Couldn't hold the massive rain shower of our feelings.
Cupid told me he helped out in issues
of love, not of stupidity.
The weather was uncontrollable, we lost the
wind and in came the humidity.
Cupid wasn't on my side,
And soon I lost my ride.
So I rode solo.

I kept my world down low,
Did my own independent things,
Made my own promises and bought my own rings
I valued myself and gave me the whole world.
If anyone tries to pursue me, he'll have
to view me as the only girl.
I'll let my guard be so strong and wait till he can crack it.
I'll let him lose his control till, my heart, he can map it.
Where did my naked heart go?
I don't know,
But just chase it.

Every day I fall deeper in love with myself,
Which makes it harder for me to
fall in love with anyone else.

2009

If You Stay, Don't Try to Change Me

If I gave you a moment of my time
And you chose to accept it,
I'd invite you deep into my mind,
But please try not to perfect it.
I'm a bit different, I'll accept it.
Your reversed perceptions,
Knotted up, are mine but with clarity.
May take them as misconceptions.
You may question my level of peculiarity.
That is okay with me as long as you stay
Long enough to listen to the other parts
Of me, which has not been exposed.
Reverse chronological order, end from when it starts.
There is more to me than my past, as I suppose.

No Need for Explanations

Sometimes I wish I could take a step back in time
Just to save some verses on my rhymes.
The pain this path has placed on me
Made me stronger, so nothing will ever faze me.
It just kills me to see true love walking away
Every single time because I know the chances of his stay
Are minimal. He always walks away
before I have a chance to say
What I have to say and explain
Myself.
Give her enough rope and she will hang herself.
That's how I used to see things because
I always found solutions, until it was
Such a confusion, where life left me.
It was a moment in time where loads were hefty.
Psychologically, every new problematic
situation is hard to handle,
Leaving craters in my memories, just enough to vandal
All particles of positivity that made up who I was.
A moment of experiencing withdrawals.
These moments in time are not easy.

After a while, you just learn how to grab the bull by its horns.

2007

Battling Depression With Company

Dear God, I'm so grateful for every waking moment.
Piece me back together, for I am just a component.
Soothe me to sleep in this melodious night,
And please don't ever lose me from sight.
Even when it's bright,
Since bright lights
Tend to dim.
Lost sight of where to swim.
Lost in a mental battle,
A horse without a saddle.
The horse can still be tamable,
Just like wrinkled sheets are still foldable.
Dear God, I ask to be more than just
a horse or wrinkled sheets.
I know how to lose, but refrain from any defeats
Because I want to choose my destiny
With you right next to me.

Enrolled in a life where constant changes are the only occurrence that is granted to portray consistency.

I do have faith in people. If I say you can do it, it is because I feel that it is possible and you have the potential to do it. It is all driven by mentality, so do not doubt my words, and especially do not doubt yourself. Take a tiny step that leads you to a nice pathway. Encouraging words psychologically mold a person's mentality for the better. Someone is always in your life to make a difference, unless you are the one to make a difference in their life.

Pressure

Let me be your motivator nearby or even far.
Let me push you because I don't want you on par
With the rest of society.
While using propriety
And humbleness to put yourself in other's shoes.
With the mindset strong enough to make moves
When the world is crumbling at your feet.
Agile enough to make moves within a beat.
Allow me to be the alarm clock that awakens
all of the senses in your soul.
You will not need the snooze button because
I'll make sure you reach your goals.
If you are not ready for intense heat, please step aside
Because I will push you till all the pressure has been applied.
I will break you in a gentle manner and
transform you to your potential.
Your list of goals and dreams will transform into credentials.
No ifs or buts, because I find solutions
to questions and problems.
I'll sit right next to you till you learn
to find ways to solve 'em.
Do not allow these actions or my
intentions to intimidate you.
I only want to get the best out of you.

The walls slowly seem to get closer without warning,
Precisely the same way life happens.
We never know what we're going to get,
Whether it is the boogie monster underneath our bed
Or the monster in our closet.
Somehow things get better when mom turns on the light,
The same way God allows the sun to shine.
In other words, do not stress; tomorrow is another day.

Yoga

Swing your body into an upward facing dog position.
Save your soul and avoid any collision.
Do not let your heart collide with this world.
Chest out, find freedom, breathe in and now curl.
Curl into the baby you once were.
Avoid any next movements that might occur.
Vulnerability, embrace it.
It is life, go ahead and face it.
But do not let any barriers stop you.
Swing to the movement and find your way
out into a downward-facing dog.
Face yourself because your body and your
subconscious must have this dialogue.
Shift your center of gravity and use your core.
From you, life will always ask for more
Because you are now a warrior.
Do not focus on the exterior,
Focus on the core and balance.
Stay away from negativity and malice.
This journey has been lengthy.
Filled with struggles, far from empty.
There has been a lot of pain and many tears,
But, baby, you just faced your fears.

That is why you are now a warrior with the ability to defend.
Broken bones, broken heart, and all the
things you learned to amend.
You have been that hungry dog and that vulnerable baby,
But now you are a warrior that does not need any saving.
The beauty is that you can always go back to being
that hungry dog and that vulnerable baby
Because, as warriors, we are also human,
And we forget that, which never fails to amaze me.

In this world, no one owes you anything. You cannot exceed what someone doesn't offer. Unfortunately, even if it's under foul circumstances, you can only accept what's in front of you. There's no need for begging, there is no need for expectations, and there is no need for false hope. If pain lies deep within, depend on no one for soothing. I understand myself more than anyone does. I understand my fears, my passions and my faith, and each one has been tested. Life will come to you as it is. Accept what is in front of you. Life is beautiful, which includes struggles and successes. I understand my own happiness even when it has been recently tested. I understand my pain which has led to my insecurities. I do not see my insecurities in a negative connotation. I embrace them and work on them each day to silence the baby that cries within. It is not only the positive thoughts that propel you to move forward.

You need both, the yin and the yang. You learn from these insecurities and gain the ability to understand yourself. Wounds may be fresh, but with whichever pace you decide to attempt to heal is up to you. It is not the destination, my friends, it is the journey. Enjoy the moments because they are never guaranteed.

The Bigger Picture

I'm tired of writing loving and depressing poems,
Giving power to men when I should disown 'em.
I am a queen with poise and graceful persona.
I should be on a beach, being fed grapes
while drinking a Corona.

But instead, this poem is about limitations,
Societal norms and lack of imagination.
It's about how we're suppressed on foundations
Created by dead men.
Instead, we forget we are God sent.
We each have a mind of our own,
But our mind is stuck inside this phone.
Somehow, we complain we feel alone.

Allow me to open the gateway,
But you have let go of that hearsay.
Let go of that gossip and be my protégé.
Learn that there is no such thing as limitations.
It's a societal norm created for imitation,
For you to imitate and follow the norm.
We need to get stronger after the storm,
Not weakened, allowing people to tell us what to do.
Realize that society frames you into looking like a buffoon.

Love yourself and understand that there are no limits.
We are all connected, resembling the same spirits.
Care about one another
Like sisters and brothers,
But know you are but a grain of salt in this vast universe.
Knowledge, from my mouth to your brain it will immerse.

With that said, your thoughts have
the power to manifest itself.
Protect the mind, body, and soul by wearing a seat belt,
Using positive thoughts and positive vibes.
Listen to your intuition as it guides
You to your limitless opportunities that have been blocked
By society taking away your confidence that's locked
Away from your reach.
Wanting to use bleach
To whiten your skin.
Use what's built within
And be comfortable with your skin.
It's not about appearances,
So limit the interferences
In wavelength.
Magnitude measured by strength.
Let yourself shine
To the divine.
Attract what is fine
And listen to the signs
That are made specifically for you.
Please believe, because your dreams will come true.

*H*alfway into week five: swimming in an ocean of work without the ability to touch the ground or sight of shore. I swim, having a great deal of endurance, but still no sight of land. My body gets weak and weary; I drown.

Setting Boundaries

People will speak their projection of themselves on to you.
The whole world is going to label you
Whether you live your life or not, but
you gotta live your own truth.
Set boundaries, get wild, get lost to find
yourself and enjoy your youth
Because age is nothing but a mindset; perceive
yourself as a God or a Goddess
Because source energy and God resides
within you, so don't be modest.
Jesus lived his life, had fun with Mary Magdalene,
a prostitute, was betrayed time after time.
He didn't judge, but he enjoyed a full
life turning water into wine.
Whether you believe in Jesus or not,
we were not meant to judge.
Even though it's not the easiest thing to
do, let go of the hatred and grudge.
From now on, I will dedicate my time to love
even if it doesn't lead to the expected path.
I'll make sure to handle the aftermath.
But at this moment, I have love for
everyone, even if you hurt me.
Even if you don't reciprocate the love, this is my journey!

Independence

The bad part about being independent
is that you need no one.
But I have been in such a perpetual high,
constantly getting things done,
That I've been alone for so long and no
one summons my love anymore.
Not that they haven't tried, the thing is
that I've lost the urgency to explore.
A map full lost hopes and dreams
Because that is all they can offer, at least that's what it seems.
I'm much happier solely depending on me.
I trust me, I love me and, at this point,
no one can destroy me.
At this point, my compass points at me!
I have found me; I've discovered the richness of me.
Who would I allow to enjoy my richness?
Who is going to be my partner? My witness
Of aging lines, stretch marks and
financial and spiritual growth?
Who am I to share this oath?
If no one attracts me, then I've lost hope.

I be lovin' people

I be lovin' people
Like I genuinely fall deeply in love with people.
In a very sincere platonic manner,
Like I love people up to such standard
Of knowing that I can love deeper each time.
Knowing that action was done with a heart that's mine.
I be loving people.
Before I loved with an ego, that love came
from a place of needing love.
See, now I love from a place of love,
Not needing anything in return.
Maybe when seeing a frown, I'll turn
It to a 180-degree angle
And let our thoughts get tangled.
By listening to how our days have been
Or speaking about scrambled thoughts
or just a simple check-in.
I be lovin' people,
Not caring about your background,
your sins, poverty or wealth.
God said: love your neighbor as you love yourself.

So, the next time you see me, let me love you
In these hard times because I see what you've been through.
I try to send random messages here and there
As a reminder that you're on my mind and I care.
Let me love you.
I feel like it isn't common to say I love you.
To all my friends, I love you.
Don't be frightened if I say I miss you.
I'm proud of you.
I'm here to listen whenever you're ready.
You need someone? I am here already.
I be lovin' people. Don't you forget that!

2008